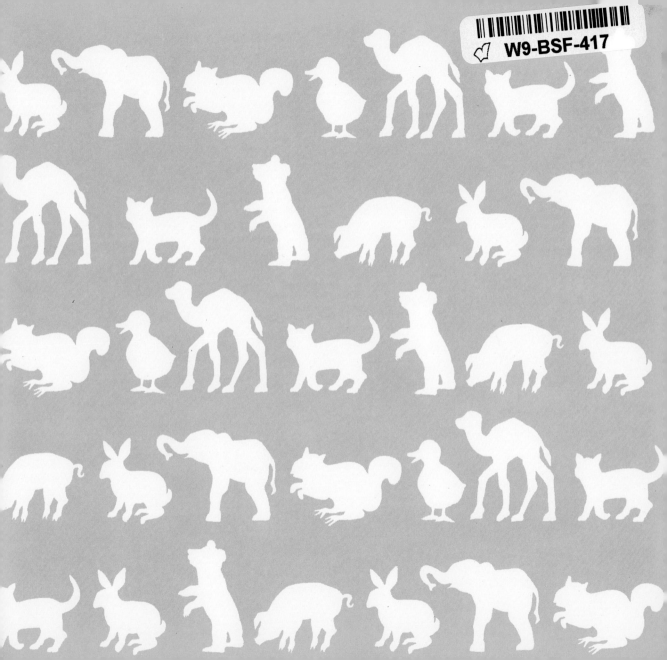

LADYBIRD BOOKS, INC.
Auburn, Maine 04210 U.S.A.
© LADYBIRD BOOKS LTD MCMLXXXVIII
Loughborough, Leicestershire, England

Printed in England

Baby Forest Animals

by RONNE PELTZMAN RANDALL
illustrated by GWEN TOURRET

Ladybird Books

Baby squirrel lives high
in a leafy treetop.
Who has come to visit him?

Three baby foxes have come
out of their den.
Have they heard a noise?
What can it be?

Mother bear has caught
a fish for her cubs.

Mother deer knows
her fawn will wait for her
on his cozy bed of leaves.

Baby chipmunk has found
a crunchy nut to munch.

Baby raccoon will soon learn
to wash her food in the stream.

Mother beaver gives
her tired baby a ride.

The baby skunks
explore their forest home.

The baby porcupines
see their mother coming
over the mossy ground.

The baby weasels have found
a cool and shady place to play.

Baby hedgehog has stopped to rest
under a toadstool.

Mother mouse watches over her sleeping babies.

The baby owls
are awake at night.
In the morning
they will go to sleep.